50 Sugar Drink Recipes

By: Kelly Johnson

Table of Contents

- Classic Lemonade
- Strawberry Lemonade
- Mint Mojito Lemonade
- Raspberry Limeade
- Tropical Punch
- Pineapple Coconut Cooler
- Orange Creamsicle Drink
- Watermelon Fizz
- Peach Iced Tea
- Mango Lemonade
- Blueberry Lemonade
- Cherry Limeade
- Ginger Ale Punch
- Apple Cinnamon Cider
- Cranberry Sparkler
- Blackberry Mint Fizz
- Lemon Basil Sparkler
- Lime Coconut Water
- Spiced Apple Cider
- Pomegranate Lemonade
- Peach Mint Iced Tea
- Tropical Fruit Punch
- Watermelon Mint Cooler
- Grape Lemonade
- Strawberry Kiwi Lemonade
- Coconut Water Lemonade
- Iced Coffee with Vanilla Syrup
- Iced Caramel Macchiato
- Classic Root Beer Float
- Cherry Peach Fizz
- Lemon Ginger Iced Tea
- Tropical Fruit Smoothie
- Lemon and Honey Water
- Kiwi Strawberry Smoothie
- Coconut Lime Cooler

- Lime Mojito Cooler
- Berry Lemonade Slush
- Frozen Peach Drink
- Mango Coconut Smoothie
- Pineapple Ginger Punch
- Blueberry Mojito
- Pomegranate Mint Cooler
- Cucumber Lemonade
- Sweet Tea Lemonade
- Raspberry Coconut Cooler
- Strawberry Mint Fizz
- Pineapple Mint Slush
- Lemon Poppy Seed Fizz
- Grapefruit Honey Sparkler
- Cantaloupe Mint Cooler

Classic Lemonade

Ingredients:

- 1 cup of freshly squeezed lemon juice (about 4-6 lemons)
- 1 cup of granulated sugar
- 5 cups of cold water
- Ice cubes
- Lemon slices for garnish (optional)

Instructions:

1. **Make the Simple Syrup:** In a small saucepan, combine 1 cup of water and the sugar. Heat over medium heat, stirring until the sugar is completely dissolved. Set aside to cool.
2. **Juice the Lemons:** While the syrup is cooling, cut your lemons in half and juice them. Strain the juice to remove seeds and pulp for a smooth lemonade.
3. **Combine Lemon Juice and Syrup:** In a large pitcher, add the lemon juice and simple syrup. Stir to combine.
4. **Add Cold Water:** Pour in the remaining 4 cups of cold water and stir to mix. Taste and adjust sweetness by adding more water or sugar if desired.
5. **Chill and Serve:** Add ice cubes to the pitcher, stir again, and serve in glasses. Garnish with lemon slices if desired.

Strawberry Lemonade

Ingredients:

- 1 cup of fresh strawberries, hulled
- 1 cup of freshly squeezed lemon juice
- 1 cup of granulated sugar
- 5 cups of cold water
- Ice cubes
- Strawberry slices for garnish (optional)

Instructions:

1. Blend the strawberries until smooth.
2. In a small saucepan, make simple syrup by combining sugar and 1 cup of water, heating until dissolved.
3. In a pitcher, combine the lemon juice, strawberry puree, and syrup.
4. Add 4 cups of cold water, stir well, and chill with ice.
5. Serve in glasses with strawberry slices.

Mint Mojito Lemonade

Ingredients:

- 1 cup of freshly squeezed lemon juice
- 1/2 cup of fresh mint leaves
- 1 cup of granulated sugar
- 5 cups of cold water
- Ice cubes
- Mint sprigs for garnish (optional)

Instructions:

1. Muddle the mint leaves with sugar in a large pitcher.
2. Add lemon juice and stir to dissolve the sugar.
3. Pour in the cold water, stir, and add ice.
4. Garnish with mint sprigs and serve chilled.

Raspberry Limeade

Ingredients:

- 1 cup of fresh raspberries
- 1/2 cup of freshly squeezed lime juice
- 1 cup of granulated sugar
- 5 cups of cold water
- Ice cubes
- Lime slices for garnish (optional)

Instructions:

1. Puree the raspberries in a blender and strain.
2. In a saucepan, make a simple syrup by dissolving sugar in 1 cup of water.
3. Mix the raspberry puree, lime juice, syrup, and 4 cups of water in a pitcher.
4. Serve over ice with lime slices.

Tropical Punch

Ingredients:

- 1 cup of pineapple juice
- 1 cup of orange juice
- 1/2 cup of coconut water
- 1/4 cup of freshly squeezed lime juice
- 1 cup of club soda
- Ice cubes
- Pineapple slices for garnish (optional)

Instructions:

1. Mix the pineapple juice, orange juice, coconut water, and lime juice in a pitcher.
2. Add club soda and stir gently.
3. Serve over ice and garnish with pineapple slices.

Pineapple Coconut Cooler

Ingredients:

- 1 cup of pineapple juice
- 1/2 cup of coconut milk
- 1 tablespoon of honey (optional)
- 5 cups of cold water
- Ice cubes
- Pineapple chunks for garnish (optional)

Instructions:

1. Mix the pineapple juice, coconut milk, and honey in a blender until smooth.
2. Pour the mixture into a pitcher and add cold water.
3. Stir well, chill, and serve with ice cubes and pineapple chunks.

Orange Creamsicle Drink

Ingredients:

- 1 cup of orange juice
- 1/2 cup of vanilla ice cream
- 1 cup of milk
- 1 tablespoon of honey (optional)
- Ice cubes

Instructions:

1. Blend the orange juice, vanilla ice cream, milk, and honey until smooth.
2. Pour into glasses, add ice cubes, and serve chilled.

Watermelon Fizz

Ingredients:

- 2 cups of fresh watermelon chunks
- 1/2 cup of freshly squeezed lime juice
- 1 cup of club soda
- 1 tablespoon of honey or sugar
- Ice cubes
- Watermelon wedges for garnish (optional)

Instructions:

1. Puree the watermelon in a blender and strain.
2. Mix the watermelon juice, lime juice, and sweetener in a pitcher.
3. Add club soda and stir gently.
4. Serve over ice with watermelon wedges.

Peach Iced Tea

Ingredients:

- 3 black tea bags
- 2 ripe peaches, peeled and sliced
- 1/4 cup of honey (or sugar to taste)
- 5 cups of boiling water
- Ice cubes
- Peach slices for garnish (optional)

Instructions:

1. Brew the tea bags in 5 cups of boiling water and let cool.
2. Puree the peaches and strain.
3. Mix the tea with peach puree and honey.
4. Serve over ice with peach slices.

Mango Lemonade

Ingredients:

- 1 cup of fresh mango puree
- 1 cup of freshly squeezed lemon juice
- 1 cup of granulated sugar
- 5 cups of cold water
- Ice cubes
- Mango slices for garnish (optional)

Instructions:

1. Blend the mangoes until smooth.
2. In a small saucepan, make simple syrup by dissolving sugar in 1 cup of water.
3. Combine mango puree, lemon juice, syrup, and cold water in a pitcher.
4. Stir well, serve with ice, and garnish with mango slices.

Blueberry Lemonade

Ingredients:

- 1 cup of fresh blueberries
- 1 cup of freshly squeezed lemon juice
- 1 cup of granulated sugar
- 5 cups of cold water
- Ice cubes
- Lemon slices for garnish (optional)

Instructions:

1. Puree the blueberries in a blender and strain to remove the skins.
2. In a saucepan, dissolve the sugar in 1 cup of water to make simple syrup.
3. In a pitcher, combine the lemon juice, blueberry puree, and simple syrup.
4. Add the remaining cold water and stir well.
5. Serve over ice and garnish with lemon slices.

Cherry Limeade

Ingredients:

- 1 cup of fresh cherries, pitted
- 1/2 cup of freshly squeezed lime juice
- 1 cup of granulated sugar
- 5 cups of cold water
- Ice cubes
- Lime slices and cherries for garnish (optional)

Instructions:

1. Blend the cherries until smooth and strain to remove the skins.
2. In a saucepan, create a simple syrup by dissolving sugar in 1 cup of water.
3. In a pitcher, combine the lime juice, cherry puree, and simple syrup.
4. Add 4 cups of cold water and stir well.
5. Serve over ice and garnish with lime slices and cherries.

Ginger Ale Punch

Ingredients:

- 4 cups of ginger ale
- 2 cups of pineapple juice
- 1 cup of orange juice
- 1 tablespoon of lime juice
- Ice cubes
- Orange and lime slices for garnish (optional)

Instructions:

1. In a large pitcher, combine ginger ale, pineapple juice, orange juice, and lime juice.
2. Stir gently to combine and add ice cubes.
3. Serve chilled and garnish with orange and lime slices.

Apple Cinnamon Cider

Ingredients:

- 4 cups of apple cider
- 1 cinnamon stick
- 1 tablespoon of honey (optional)
- 1/2 cup of water
- Apple slices for garnish (optional)

Instructions:

1. In a saucepan, heat the apple cider and water over medium heat.
2. Add the cinnamon stick and honey, stirring until the honey dissolves.
3. Let simmer for 5-10 minutes, then remove from heat.
4. Serve warm or chilled, garnished with apple slices.

Cranberry Sparkler

Ingredients:

- 1 cup of cranberry juice
- 1/2 cup of club soda
- 1 tablespoon of freshly squeezed lime juice
- 1 tablespoon of sugar (optional)
- Ice cubes
- Fresh cranberries for garnish (optional)

Instructions:

1. In a pitcher, combine cranberry juice, lime juice, and sugar (if using).
2. Add club soda and stir gently.
3. Serve over ice and garnish with fresh cranberries.

Blackberry Mint Fizz

Ingredients:

- 1 cup of fresh blackberries
- 1/2 cup of fresh mint leaves
- 1 tablespoon of sugar
- 1/2 cup of freshly squeezed lime juice
- 3 cups of club soda
- Ice cubes
- Mint sprigs for garnish (optional)

Instructions:

1. Muddle the blackberries, mint leaves, and sugar in a pitcher.
2. Add the lime juice and stir to combine.
3. Pour in the club soda and stir gently.
4. Serve over ice and garnish with mint sprigs.

Lemon Basil Sparkler

Ingredients:

- 1 cup of freshly squeezed lemon juice
- 1/2 cup of fresh basil leaves
- 1 tablespoon of honey or sugar
- 3 cups of sparkling water
- Ice cubes
- Lemon slices for garnish (optional)

Instructions:

1. Muddle the basil leaves with honey or sugar in a pitcher.
2. Add lemon juice and stir until combined.
3. Pour in the sparkling water and stir gently.
4. Serve over ice and garnish with lemon slices.

Lime Coconut Water

Ingredients:

- 2 cups of coconut water
- 1/2 cup of freshly squeezed lime juice
- 1 tablespoon of honey (optional)
- Ice cubes
- Lime slices for garnish (optional)

Instructions:

1. In a pitcher, combine coconut water, lime juice, and honey (if using).
2. Stir to combine and chill in the refrigerator.
3. Serve over ice and garnish with lime slices.

Spiced Apple Cider

Ingredients:

- 4 cups of apple cider
- 2 cinnamon sticks
- 3-4 cloves
- 1 tablespoon of honey or brown sugar (optional)
- 1 orange, sliced (optional)
- Apple slices for garnish (optional)

Instructions:

1. In a saucepan, combine apple cider, cinnamon sticks, cloves, and honey (if using).
2. Heat over medium heat until simmering. Let it simmer for 10-15 minutes to infuse the spices.
3. Remove from heat and discard the cinnamon sticks and cloves.
4. Serve warm, garnished with orange slices and apple slices.

Pomegranate Lemonade

Ingredients:

- 1 cup of pomegranate juice
- 1 cup of freshly squeezed lemon juice
- 1 cup of granulated sugar
- 4 cups of cold water
- Ice cubes
- Pomegranate seeds and lemon slices for garnish (optional)

Instructions:

1. In a small saucepan, dissolve sugar in 1 cup of water to make a simple syrup.
2. In a large pitcher, combine the pomegranate juice, lemon juice, and simple syrup.
3. Add the remaining cold water and stir well.
4. Serve over ice and garnish with pomegranate seeds and lemon slices.

Peach Mint Iced Tea

Ingredients:

- 3 black tea bags
- 2 ripe peaches, peeled and sliced
- 1/4 cup of fresh mint leaves
- 1/4 cup of honey or sugar (optional)
- 4 cups of boiling water
- Ice cubes
- Mint sprigs for garnish (optional)

Instructions:

1. Brew the tea bags in 4 cups of boiling water and let it cool.
2. Blend the peaches with honey or sugar until smooth and strain.
3. In a pitcher, combine the brewed tea, peach puree, and mint leaves.
4. Stir well and serve over ice, garnished with mint sprigs.

Tropical Fruit Punch

Ingredients:

- 1 cup of pineapple juice
- 1 cup of orange juice
- 1/2 cup of mango juice
- 1/2 cup of coconut water
- 1 tablespoon of freshly squeezed lime juice
- Ice cubes
- Tropical fruit slices (pineapple, mango, orange) for garnish (optional)

Instructions:

1. In a large pitcher, combine pineapple juice, orange juice, mango juice, coconut water, and lime juice.
2. Stir gently and serve over ice.
3. Garnish with tropical fruit slices.

Watermelon Mint Cooler

Ingredients:

- 3 cups of fresh watermelon chunks
- 1/4 cup of fresh mint leaves
- 1 tablespoon of honey (optional)
- 1 tablespoon of freshly squeezed lime juice
- 4 cups of cold water
- Ice cubes
- Mint sprigs for garnish (optional)

Instructions:

1. Puree the watermelon in a blender and strain to remove pulp.
2. Muddle the mint leaves with honey and lime juice in a pitcher.
3. Add the watermelon juice and cold water to the pitcher, and stir well.
4. Serve over ice and garnish with mint sprigs.

Grape Lemonade

Ingredients:

- 1 cup of fresh grape juice
- 1 cup of freshly squeezed lemon juice
- 1 cup of granulated sugar
- 4 cups of cold water
- Ice cubes
- Lemon slices for garnish (optional)

Instructions:

1. In a small saucepan, make a simple syrup by dissolving sugar in 1 cup of water.
2. In a large pitcher, combine the grape juice, lemon juice, and simple syrup.
3. Add the remaining cold water and stir well.
4. Serve over ice and garnish with lemon slices.

Strawberry Kiwi Lemonade

Ingredients:

- 1 cup of fresh strawberries, hulled
- 2 ripe kiwis, peeled
- 1 cup of freshly squeezed lemon juice
- 1 cup of granulated sugar
- 4 cups of cold water
- Ice cubes
- Strawberry and kiwi slices for garnish (optional)

Instructions:

1. Blend the strawberries and kiwis until smooth, and strain to remove pulp.
2. In a small saucepan, make simple syrup by dissolving sugar in 1 cup of water.
3. In a pitcher, combine the lemon juice, strawberry-kiwi puree, and syrup.
4. Add the remaining cold water and stir well.
5. Serve over ice and garnish with strawberry and kiwi slices.

Coconut Water Lemonade

Ingredients:

- 2 cups of coconut water
- 1 cup of freshly squeezed lemon juice
- 1/2 cup of honey or agave syrup
- 4 cups of cold water
- Ice cubes
- Lemon slices for garnish (optional)

Instructions:

1. In a small saucepan, dissolve honey or agave syrup in 1 cup of water to make a simple syrup.
2. In a large pitcher, combine coconut water, lemon juice, and simple syrup.
3. Add the remaining cold water and stir well.
4. Serve over ice and garnish with lemon slices.

Iced Coffee with Vanilla Syrup

Ingredients:

- 2 cups of brewed coffee (chilled)
- 1/4 cup of vanilla syrup
- 1/2 cup of milk or cream (optional)
- Ice cubes
- Coffee beans for garnish (optional)

Instructions:

1. Brew the coffee and chill it in the refrigerator.
2. In a glass, combine chilled coffee with vanilla syrup and stir well.
3. Add milk or cream if desired.
4. Serve over ice and garnish with coffee beans.

Iced Caramel Macchiato

Ingredients:

- 1 cup of freshly brewed espresso (or strong coffee)
- 1/2 cup of milk (whole or any preference)
- 2 tablespoons of caramel syrup
- Ice cubes
- Whipped cream (optional)

Instructions:

1. Brew the espresso and allow it to cool slightly.
2. Fill a glass with ice cubes and pour in the caramel syrup.
3. Add the cooled espresso to the glass, followed by the milk.
4. Stir gently to combine, and top with whipped cream if desired.
5. Serve immediately and enjoy the rich flavors!

Classic Root Beer Float

Ingredients:

- 1 bottle or can of root beer
- 2 scoops of vanilla ice cream
- Whipped cream (optional)
- Maraschino cherry (optional)

Instructions:

1. Place two scoops of vanilla ice cream in a tall glass.
2. Pour root beer over the ice cream slowly to avoid foam overflow.
3. Top with whipped cream and a maraschino cherry if desired.
4. Serve with a straw and enjoy the classic, fizzy treat!

Cherry Peach Fizz

Ingredients:

- 1/2 cup of cherry juice
- 1/2 cup of peach juice
- 1 tablespoon of freshly squeezed lime juice
- 1 cup of sparkling water
- Ice cubes
- Lime slices for garnish (optional)

Instructions:

1. In a glass, combine the cherry juice, peach juice, and lime juice.
2. Add ice cubes and top with sparkling water.
3. Stir gently and garnish with lime slices if desired.
4. Serve chilled and enjoy the fruity fizz!

Lemon Ginger Iced Tea

Ingredients:

- 3 black tea bags
- 1-inch piece of fresh ginger, sliced
- 2 tablespoons of honey or sugar (optional)
- 1/2 cup of freshly squeezed lemon juice
- Ice cubes
- Lemon slices and ginger slices for garnish (optional)

Instructions:

1. Brew the tea bags in 4 cups of boiling water and add the sliced ginger.
2. Let the tea steep for 5-7 minutes, then remove the tea bags.
3. Stir in honey or sugar (if using) and let the tea cool.
4. Add lemon juice and serve the tea over ice cubes.
5. Garnish with lemon and ginger slices for extra flavor.

Tropical Fruit Smoothie

Ingredients:

- 1/2 cup of pineapple chunks
- 1/2 cup of mango chunks
- 1/2 cup of banana slices
- 1/2 cup of coconut water
- 1/4 cup of Greek yogurt (optional)
- Ice cubes

Instructions:

1. Combine pineapple, mango, banana, coconut water, and yogurt in a blender.
2. Blend until smooth and creamy.
3. Add ice cubes to thicken the smoothie, then blend again.
4. Pour into a glass and serve chilled for a tropical delight.

Lemon and Honey Water

Ingredients:

- 1 cup of warm water
- 1 tablespoon of honey
- 1 tablespoon of freshly squeezed lemon juice
- Lemon slices for garnish (optional)

Instructions:

1. In a mug, mix warm water with honey until dissolved.
2. Add lemon juice and stir.
3. Serve with a few lemon slices for garnish, and enjoy a refreshing, soothing drink.

Kiwi Strawberry Smoothie

Ingredients:

- 2 ripe kiwis, peeled
- 1/2 cup of fresh strawberries, hulled
- 1/2 cup of almond milk (or any milk preference)
- 1 tablespoon of honey or agave syrup (optional)
- Ice cubes

Instructions:

1. Blend the kiwis, strawberries, almond milk, and honey in a blender.
2. Add ice cubes to thicken and blend until smooth.
3. Pour into a glass and serve immediately for a vibrant, healthy smoothie.

Coconut Lime Cooler

Ingredients:

- 1 cup of coconut water
- 1 tablespoon of freshly squeezed lime juice
- 1 teaspoon of honey or agave syrup (optional)
- Ice cubes
- Lime slices for garnish (optional)

Instructions:

1. In a glass, combine coconut water, lime juice, and honey (if using).
2. Stir well and serve over ice cubes.
3. Garnish with lime slices for a refreshing, tropical experience.

Lime Mojito Cooler

Ingredients:

- 1/4 cup of fresh lime juice
- 10-12 fresh mint leaves
- 1 tablespoon of sugar or simple syrup
- 1 cup of soda water
- Ice cubes
- Lime slices and mint sprigs for garnish

Instructions:

1. Muddle the mint leaves and sugar (or syrup) in the bottom of a glass.
2. Add fresh lime juice and stir to combine.
3. Fill the glass with ice cubes and top with soda water.
4. Stir gently and garnish with lime slices and mint sprigs.

Berry Lemonade Slush

Ingredients:

- 1 cup of mixed berries (strawberries, blueberries, raspberries)
- 1 cup of freshly squeezed lemon juice
- 1/4 cup of honey or sugar (optional)
- 3 cups of ice cubes
- Lemon slices and berries for garnish (optional)

Instructions:

1. In a blender, combine the mixed berries, lemon juice, and honey or sugar.
2. Add the ice cubes and blend until smooth and slushy.
3. Serve in glasses, garnished with lemon slices and berries for a refreshing treat.

Frozen Peach Drink

Ingredients:

- 2 cups of frozen peach slices
- 1/2 cup of orange juice
- 1/4 cup of coconut water
- 1 tablespoon of honey or agave syrup (optional)
- Ice cubes (if needed)

Instructions:

1. Blend the frozen peaches, orange juice, coconut water, and honey until smooth.
2. If the mixture is too thick, add a few ice cubes to help blend.
3. Pour into a glass and serve chilled for a tropical frozen treat.

Mango Coconut Smoothie

Ingredients:

- 1 ripe mango, peeled and chopped
- 1/2 cup of coconut milk
- 1/2 cup of Greek yogurt
- 1 tablespoon of honey (optional)
- Ice cubes

Instructions:

1. Combine the mango, coconut milk, Greek yogurt, and honey in a blender.
2. Add ice cubes and blend until smooth.
3. Pour into a glass and serve for a creamy, tropical smoothie.

Pineapple Ginger Punch

Ingredients:

- 2 cups of fresh pineapple juice
- 1 tablespoon of freshly grated ginger
- 1 tablespoon of honey or sugar (optional)
- 1/2 cup of sparkling water
- Ice cubes
- Pineapple slices and mint leaves for garnish (optional)

Instructions:

1. In a pitcher, combine pineapple juice, grated ginger, and honey or sugar.
2. Stir until the honey or sugar dissolves.
3. Add ice cubes and top with sparkling water.
4. Serve in glasses, garnished with pineapple slices and mint leaves for a refreshing punch.

Blueberry Mojito

Ingredients:

- 1/2 cup of fresh blueberries
- 1/4 cup of fresh mint leaves
- 1 tablespoon of sugar or simple syrup
- 1 tablespoon of lime juice
- 1 cup of soda water
- Ice cubes
- Lime slices and mint sprigs for garnish

Instructions:

1. Muddle the blueberries, mint leaves, and sugar or simple syrup in a glass.
2. Add lime juice and ice cubes, and stir well.
3. Top with soda water and garnish with lime slices and mint sprigs for a fizzy, fruity twist on a mojito.

Pomegranate Mint Cooler

Ingredients:

- 1 cup of pomegranate juice
- 1/4 cup of fresh mint leaves
- 1 tablespoon of honey or agave syrup (optional)
- 1 cup of soda water
- Ice cubes
- Pomegranate seeds and mint sprigs for garnish

Instructions:

1. Muddle the mint leaves with honey or agave syrup in a glass.
2. Add the pomegranate juice and stir.
3. Add ice cubes and top with soda water.
4. Garnish with pomegranate seeds and mint sprigs for a refreshing cooler.

Cucumber Lemonade

Ingredients:

- 1 cucumber, peeled and sliced
- 1 cup of freshly squeezed lemon juice
- 1/4 cup of honey or sugar (optional)
- 4 cups of cold water
- Ice cubes
- Cucumber slices and lemon wedges for garnish

Instructions:

1. In a blender, combine cucumber slices, lemon juice, and honey or sugar.
2. Blend until smooth and strain to remove the pulp.
3. In a pitcher, mix the cucumber lemonade with cold water and stir well.
4. Serve over ice, garnished with cucumber slices and lemon wedges.

Sweet Tea Lemonade

Ingredients:

- 2 cups of brewed black tea (cooled)
- 1 cup of freshly squeezed lemon juice
- 1/4 cup of sugar (or to taste)
- 1-2 cups of cold water
- Ice cubes
- Lemon slices for garnish

Instructions:

1. Brew the black tea and let it cool.
2. In a pitcher, combine the cooled tea, lemon juice, and sugar. Stir well until the sugar dissolves.
3. Add cold water to adjust the strength to your preference.
4. Serve over ice cubes and garnish with lemon slices for a sweet and tangy beverage.

Raspberry Coconut Cooler

Ingredients:

- 1 cup of fresh raspberries
- 1/2 cup of coconut milk
- 1 tablespoon of honey or agave syrup (optional)
- 1 cup of sparkling water
- Ice cubes
- Fresh raspberries for garnish (optional)

Instructions:

1. Blend fresh raspberries, coconut milk, and honey (if using) until smooth.
2. Add ice cubes to a glass and pour the raspberry coconut mixture over.
3. Top with sparkling water and stir gently.
4. Garnish with fresh raspberries for a tropical, berry-filled drink.

Strawberry Mint Fizz

Ingredients:

- 1 cup of fresh strawberries, hulled
- 10-12 fresh mint leaves
- 1 tablespoon of honey or sugar (optional)
- 1 cup of sparkling water
- Ice cubes
- Mint sprigs and strawberry slices for garnish

Instructions:

1. Muddle the strawberries, mint leaves, and honey (if using) in a glass.
2. Add ice cubes and top with sparkling water.
3. Stir gently and garnish with mint sprigs and strawberry slices for a bubbly, refreshing drink.

Pineapple Mint Slush

Ingredients:

- 2 cups of frozen pineapple chunks
- 1/4 cup of fresh mint leaves
- 1/4 cup of coconut water
- 1 tablespoon of honey or agave syrup (optional)
- Ice cubes

Instructions:

1. In a blender, combine frozen pineapple, mint leaves, coconut water, and honey (if using).
2. Blend until smooth and slushy.
3. Serve immediately in a chilled glass for a cool and refreshing slush.

Lemon Poppy Seed Fizz

Ingredients:

- 1 tablespoon of fresh lemon juice
- 1 tablespoon of poppy seeds
- 1 teaspoon of honey or sugar (optional)
- 1 cup of sparkling water
- Ice cubes
- Lemon slices for garnish

Instructions:

1. In a glass, combine lemon juice, poppy seeds, and honey (if using).
2. Add ice cubes and top with sparkling water.
3. Stir gently to combine and garnish with lemon slices for a light and fizzy treat.

Grapefruit Honey Sparkler

Ingredients:

- 1/2 cup of freshly squeezed grapefruit juice
- 1 tablespoon of honey
- 1 cup of sparkling water
- Ice cubes
- Grapefruit slices for garnish

Instructions:

1. In a glass, mix the grapefruit juice and honey until the honey dissolves.
2. Add ice cubes and top with sparkling water.
3. Stir gently and garnish with grapefruit slices for a tangy, fizzy drink.

Cantaloupe Mint Cooler

Ingredients:

- 2 cups of fresh cantaloupe chunks
- 10-12 fresh mint leaves
- 1 tablespoon of honey or agave syrup (optional)
- 1 cup of cold water
- Ice cubes
- Mint sprigs for garnish

Instructions:

1. Blend cantaloupe chunks, mint leaves, honey (if using), and cold water until smooth.
2. Serve over ice cubes for a cool, hydrating drink.
3. Garnish with mint sprigs for a refreshing, aromatic touch.